THE PRACTICAL STRATEGIES SERIES
IN GIFTED EDUCATION

series editors
FRANCES A. KARNES & KRISTEN R. STEPHENS

Science Strategies for Students With Gifts and Talents

Michael S. Matthews, Ph.D.

Routledge
Taylor & Francis Group

NEW YORK AND LONDON

First published 2012 by Prufrock Press Inc.

Published 2021 by Routledge
605 Third Avenue, New York, NY 10017
2 Park Square, Milton Park, Abingdon, Oxon OX14 4RN

Routledge is an imprint of the Taylor & Francis Group, an informa business

ISBN 13: 978-1-59363-891-7 (pbk)

Contents

The Practical Strategies Series in Gifted Education offers teachers, counselors, administrators, parents, and other interested parties up-to-date instructional techniques and information on a variety of issues pertinent to the field of gifted education. Each guide addresses a focused topic and is written by an individual with authority on the issue. Several guides have been published. Among the titles are:

- *Acceleration Strategies for Teaching Gifted Learners*
- *Curriculum Compacting: An Easy Start to Differentiating for High-Potential Students*
- *Enrichment Opportunities for Gifted Learners*
- *Independent Study for Gifted Learners*
- *Motivating Gifted Learners*
- *Questioning Strategies for Teaching the Gifted*
- *Social & Emotional Teaching Strategies*

For a current listing of available guides within the series, please visit Prufrock Press at http://www.prufrock.com.

Introduction

Ask adults about their experiences with learning science in school, and one is likely to hear vivid stories in response. Some may recall their reaction to dissecting a frog, their memories of growing bean plants, or their struggles to balance complex chemical equations. The chances are good that few, if any, of these tasks are a part of their daily adult lives and careers, but they have made an impression that persists for many years afterward. People seem to feel strongly about their encounters with science in school, whether the experiences were positive or negative.

Science teaching can lead to a lifelong fascination with learning, but, conversely, it also can lead to adults who mistrust science and who feel uncomfortable when scientific topics impact their daily lives. The goal of this volume is to help inspire students' love of learning, by providing suggestions and starting points from which teachers can develop their own effective instructional practices in science.

Three Reasons Why Good Teaching Is Important

Why is good teaching especially important in the sciences? Three interrelated reasons are commonly advanced to support the importance of science learning. Perhaps the most cited reason is an economic one—future national competitiveness in the global marketplace. The United States historically has been a global leader in most scientific fields over much of the 20th century, but this dominance is increasingly being challenged. Emerging economies in more populous countries, most notably India and China, are projected to grow at a rapid rate and possibly overtake the United States in innovation over the next few decades. Effective education in the science, technology, engineering, and mathematics (STEM) fields is regarded as the key to a future workforce that will keep the U.S. competitive, and resources are flowing toward systematic efforts in STEM education as an antidote to fears of declining U.S. competitiveness (National Science Board, 2010).

Gifted education also has cited future economic competitiveness as a primary rationale, but economic concerns are only one leg of a broader argument. A second rationale is based in ideas about what is important to the long-term success of a democratic society. Effective public education in science (and other areas) fosters an informed citizenry who will participate in civic life and make knowledgeable choices when voting about scientific and science-related issues that affect society.

Self-actualization offers a third rationale, one that is based in a humanistic rather than an economic or societal rationale. In this perspective, lifelong learning and self-understanding are the foremost beneficial outcomes of effective education in the sciences and other fields of study. This rationale for education implies that personal goals, career aspirations, and higher order thinking skills all should be important components of a sound education. What is important in this view is not knowledge acquisition alone, but rather how the individual is able to apply his or her knowledge to the self and to the surrounding world.

It seems appropriate to mention that "genius production" is probably not an appropriate goal for either science education or gifted education. All available evidence from studies of biographies of eminent achievers in the sciences (and other fields as well) suggests that a constellation of factors—including sheer luck—play a vital role in the eventual achievement of genius-level performance (see Simonton, 1999, 2003). An inappropriate education can perhaps prevent an otherwise able individual from achieving eminence, but even the best education cannot guarantee that genius-level performance will be achieved. These facts suggest that efforts to serve high-potential learners in the sciences and related STEM fields should focus on providing appropriate services to all students who can benefit from high-level instruction, and that such efforts should be inclusive rather than exclusive (National Science Board, 2010) in identifying who may benefit from advanced instruction.

The Organization of This Volume

This volume begins with a concise overview of the characteristics of scientifically gifted students and a consideration of the sorts of behaviors that these learners may display in the classroom. Although the preferred term at present for these learners is *students with gifts and talents in science*, at times less cumbersome phrases such as *high-ability science learners* or *scientifically gifted students*, as well as more general terms like *academically talented learners*, are used to indicate the same general group of children. The reader should not assume from the use of these alternate phrasings that giftedness is a fixed or inherited trait; rather, high potential and hard work interact over time in a developmental manner (Simonton, 1999, 2003) to yield high achievement in the sciences as well as in other fields of human endeavor.

After providing an overview of what talent in science looks like, the book moves into a discussion of teaching practices and instructional strategies that best address the needs of these learners in K–12 classrooms—beginning with a broad consideration of appropriate instructional climates and moving into some general principles that guide effective science instruction and its content. An additional section narrows further into an examination of specific instructional models and strategies that are effective in the science classroom.

The next sections address specific concerns in science instruction at varying levels of schooling: elementary, middle, and high school. These sections briefly discuss potential concerns about science instruction as observed at these different levels, with suggestions as to how instruction at each level might be improved based on the general principles presented previously. A final section sums up the arguments made throughout, and the volume concludes with selected resources and suggestions for additional reading on these topics.

The reader should be aware that although it would be possible to cite sources in support of nearly every sentence in this volume, the use of citations has been consciously limited in order to strike a more conversational tone. Using the reference and resource listings and the text as guidelines, any reference librarian will be able to point the reader toward additional research articles and books on specific topics that are of interest.

Although this guide is aimed primarily at teachers, it will also be of use to school administrators, parents of academically able learners, and others who wish to encourage growth and learning in science. Teachers can (and do) make a huge difference in the lives of children, but ultimately the responsibility for success in life is distributed among the many individuals who share the environment in which children are growing toward the achievement of their potential.

What does talent in science look like? Does being identified as gifted mean a student should be placed in an advanced science classroom? If not, how can we figure out which children might benefit from higher level instruction in science? What do we even mean by higher level instruction? These are some of the vital questions that lead toward an understanding that can inform what we do in schools.

A Practical Perspective

Gifted education traditionally has operated on the assumption that some measure of global performance, such as an IQ score, offers sufficient evidence to place students who score at or above a certain level into special instructional environments where their abilities can be nurtured. This is a great idea, but as it turns out, in practice it leads to several important shortcomings. Three of these are particularly worth noting.

One shortcoming is that although a single measure administered on a single day provides good evidence for including a student in special programming, it does not necessarily provide good evidence for excluding a student from such opportunities. Any number of factors external to what the test is designed to measure can cause someone to perform poorly on a given day. Because schools' resources are limited, retesting often is subject to a delay of up to a full year, even in cases where a teacher may have good reason to believe a student's score is not a good reflection of his or her ability. To cast a wide net that does not inappropriately exclude some learners, it is preferable to offer multiple pathways into specialized educational placements. Current best practices are leaning toward more flexible grouping arrangements, in which students move in and out of advanced learning groups as their interests and learning needs dictate. However, there is not yet a consensus on what the most effective ways are to implement such flexible grouping practices within the constraints of schools' scheduling. This primarily is an issue within programs that must assign different teachers to different groups, as within-class grouping practices do not pose this scheduling problem. Further discussion of flexible grouping practices is presented in the Improving High School Instruction in Science section of this book.

A second important shortcoming is that many students' skills do not tend to be spread evenly; this is even more of a concern among high-ability learners, whose development often is asynchronous. Because of this, scores from a global measure such as an IQ test may not accurately reflect a student's ability or interest in a broad area like science or in a specific discipline like chemistry. To address this issue, tests used to identify students to participate in a specific program (e.g., an advanced Algebra I course) should be closely matched to the skills that the program requires (e.g., prealgebra problems in mathematics) rather than to a global measure of academic ability. It is well known that such matching represents a best practice, but schools have been slow to match assessment practices closely to coursework requirements, and many gifted programs continue to rely on a global measure to identify students to participate in programming that is far narrower in scope.

Whereas the best measure of future performance is a person's prior performance in that same area, standardized test results can be nearly as useful provided they are matched carefully to the skills needed to succeed in that area. In answer to the question posed at the beginning of this section, being identified as gifted *does not* mean a student automatically should be placed in an advanced science classroom, although it suggests that he or she likely has many of the related skills necessary to succeed in that placement. Conversely, not being identified as gifted should not necessarily exclude a student from such placement. The student's prior performance in science, and perhaps a test that measures science ability, would be more appropriate as indicators of future success than any global measure of ability.

Assessing Ability in the Sciences

Performance in high school science coursework may be a relatively good predictor of success in similar college-level science courses. But younger learners may not have had prior coursework, or their prior work may have had very different expectations than those in the environment for which schools are trying to identify them. How might we recognize high potential in science among students at lower grade levels or with students who have had limited access to prior coursework in a specific area like environmental science or chemistry?

Lists of traits of students with talents in science, like lists of traits of students with gifts and talents in general, are based primarily on observation. Although there is not strong empirical evidence to support these traits or to relate them to achievement in specific scientific fields, they can be useful in providing a starting point from which to consider general aptitudes indicative of possible future success in the sciences. Table 1 lists some of these characteristics.

Although test scores, behavioral characteristics, and prior performance in a domain all are relatively effective predictors of future success in science coursework, they are not the only

Table 1
Selected Characteristics of Children
With High Ability in Science

1. Perceive relationships among different parts of a situation

2. Show curiosity about what makes things work

3. Use numbers often when expressing ideas

4. Express interest in science topics at a very young age

5. Make collections that show a high level of organization and detail

6. Are willing to spend long periods of time working alone

7. Place importance on learning the proper names of things

8. Are not content with simplistic explanations for how things work

9. Demonstrate persistence in science-related activities, such as working through setbacks or passing up games or other activities in favor of science learning

10. Enjoy explaining how things work to others

11. Tell stories that include science or science fiction

12. Have a strong memory for details

13. Are able to generalize from seemingly unrelated details; see the big picture

14. Are able to understand abstractions at a young age

15. Demonstrate a creative approach in projects related to science

Note. Adapted from *Encouraging Your Child's Science Talent: The Involved Parents' Guide* (p. 17), by M. S. Matthews, 2006, Waco, TX: Prufrock Press. Copyright 2006 by Prufrock Press. Adapted with permission.

factors responsible for success. As was noted earlier, luck does play a role. Invitations to work in a particular laboratory, to study under a specific professor, or even to take a course in a particular field of study are often the outcome of chance encounters or of seemingly random choices that accrue over time. Luck can't be consciously pursued, of course, but scientists as far back as Louis Pasteur have observed that chance favors the well-prepared individual.

Perhaps equally important is one's motivation to succeed; the trait of motivation is situation-specific and is not easily measured, but it can make a great difference in the outcomes achieved by different individuals who otherwise appear equally prepared. During high school, when coursework becomes more a matter of individual choice, differences in motivation really begin to have an effect on students' success. One can encourage motivated learners by avoiding undue restrictions on access to advanced coursework and by providing additional academic help (such as tutoring) for students who realize they may need extra assistance in a particular area of study in order to be successful.

Of course, motivation also is based in part on students' enjoyment of the subject matter, and it is here where effective teaching really can make a difference (Neber & Schommer-Aikins, 2002). Suggested strategies for teachers to improve student motivation are addressed in the three sections focusing on instruction in elementary, middle school, and high school in this book.

Unfortunately, the era of the isolated genius making dramatic scientific advances through sheer will and tenacity appears to be past. Although amateurs still make some important discoveries, science has become an extremely complex enterprise in which most advances today are made by teams of experts whose members each contribute their own areas of special expertise to the overall effort. Success in formal coursework and related academic study are the keys that allow a person the opportunity to participate in these collaborative efforts. An advanced degree may not be entirely necessary for entrepreneurs, many of whom do not complete their formal education (Gladwell, 2008), but training and credentials are essential for scientists working in academic and research settings. These STEM careers constitute between 3%–4% of the U.S. workforce, according to one recent estimate; although this may not seem like much, they represent hundreds of thousands of jobs that contribute far more to the economy and to human well-being than their numbers alone would suggest.

Finally, it should be noted that success in science coursework does not guarantee that a person will become an eminent scientist, just as high test scores do not guarantee success in life (as discussed in an interesting example provided by Gladwell, 2008). However, the absence of successful college or university coursework in science is likely to prevent a person from becoming a successful scientist as an adult, and high test scores strongly suggest that a given learner has the potential to master complex ideas and to learn their associated, specialized vocabulary. High test scores and strong grades as early as the middle school years also increase one's likelihood of being selected for high-level coursework in later grades and ultimately for competitive opportunities that may include college scholarships, employment opportunities, and related achievements. Some students realize this early in their education, while others may coast through school until they encounter a specific discipline that captures their attention, providing an intrinsic motivation to excel.

Motivation and the Gifted Learner

Unfortunately, a poor academic record can close doors of opportunity, just as a strong academic record may open them. Motivating students to learn may be the single most frustrating problem a teacher faces, and this is especially true for teachers working with high-ability learners, because there seems to be no logical reason why these students would not also be high achievers in the classroom. Although a growing literature base addresses the issue of underachievement among academically gifted learners (Kanevsky & Keighley, 2003; Kim, 2008; Matthews & McBee, 2007; McCoach & Siegle, 2003; Morisano & Shore, 2010) and a large literature base has addressed motivation in general (Eccles & Wigfield, 2002; Ryan & Deci, 2000), few interventions targeting underachievement have been evaluated systematically enough to conclude with any confidence that they are effective. Because research suggests that underachievement is related to attitudes toward learning, learning motivation will be discussed rather than underachievement per se. A brief overview of one useful theory of learning motivation follows. Keep in mind that there are entire university courses on learning motivation, so the interested reader is encouraged to consult any of the various books available on this important topic.

Garn, Matthews, and Jolly (2010) examined several approaches to motivation that parents reported using with their academically gifted children. These authors drew from a framework known as self-determination theory (Ryan & Deci, 2000), which classifies motivation into the three categories of intrinsic (or internal) motivation, extrinsic (or external) motivation, and amotivation (or lack of motivation). Research suggests that students identified as gifted have higher intrinsic motivation, on average, in comparison with students not identified, but at the same time it also shows that differences in motivation distinguish higher achieving from lower achieving learners within the gifted student population.

A glance at Table 2 will show that intrinsic motivation is what is desired in all learners, but there also are some forms of extrinsic motivation that are valuable. Self-determination theory (based in the work of Deci and Ryan, as described by Garn et al., 2010) further subdivides extrinsic motivation into four categories of internalization, which may be classified as either self-determined forms (*integration* and *identification*) or non–self-determined forms (known as *introjection* and *external*). In integration, there is still an external reward of some kind but the learning behavior is consistent with the individual's internal values. In identification, there is also an external reward but the behavior is personally important to the learner. In contrast, introjection involves learning because someone else values the reward, as when parents value good grades, and the external category involves rewards whose value is fully external to the individual who is receiving them.

Internal motivation and the two self-determined forms of extrinsic motivation are associated with positive academic outcomes, because each of these forms of motivation allows for individual volition or choice. In contrast, the non–self-determined forms of motivation can lead to feelings of a loss of control, which may lead learners to avoid or resist learning in response. Understanding the framework provided by self-determination theory is important, because it suggests what sorts of learning behaviors effective science curricula should be designed to

Table 2
Three Types of Learning Motivation According to Self-Determination Theory

	Intrinsic	Extrinsic	Amotivation
Where is the motivation's source?	Internal	External	External but ineffective
How many subtypes are there?	None	Four	None
Why does the student learn?	For enjoyment	For outside reward	Does not learn
How does the student explain learning motivation?	I finish my chemistry homework because it is interesting.	I finish my chemistry homework to receive an A.	I do not finish my chemistry homework.

elicit; this is further described in the three sections on improving instruction found in this book.

Connecting Identification, Motivation, and Service Delivery

The understanding that student motivation may vary widely, even within a group of learners identified as academically gifted, suggests why it is important for teachers to offer students a variety of approaches to mastering instructional content. Low motivation may dissuade a student from producing his or her best work, which may not only lead to low grades, but also may prevent the student from qualifying for gifted program services despite his or her high academic ability. Just because a student is not formally identified as gifted, does not mean that he or she should not be.

The identification process should align closely with the educational services that are being provided; for example, a math test might offer one indicator of which students would be likely to succeed in an advanced science curriculum, but it probably should not be the only measure used for this purpose. A test of scientific aptitude would be more closely aligned with the program's content, and therefore it would offer a more appropriate measure, even if a math measure also is used due to the mathematical proficiency requirements embedded within the science coursework in question.

Because of the likelihood that the identification process is not always accurate, some students who were not formally identified as gifted still may be able to benefit from advanced instruction in the sciences. There is some tension surrounding the issue of whether advanced instruction should be made available to all learners, even though in practice not all learners will be able or willing to take advantage of it (see comments on Advanced Placement in the Improving High School Instruction in Science section). To the extent feasible, when students are grouped for instruction, grouping practices should be sufficiently flexible so that students can move into (or out of) advanced groups as their needs and interests dictate. Elementary scheduling practices vary greatly from those in high school, so this flexibility will look somewhat different depending on the specific setting in question.

Science, Science Learning, and Advanced Learners

After considering how we might identify students who are able to benefit from special science programming, what sort of programming is this? What exactly is science, and how should we teach the competencies that it involves? Fortunately, there are a number of resources available that help to answer these questions.

What Do We Mean by Science, Anyway?

The National Science Teachers Association (NSTA) offers position statements on many important issues related to science education. The NSTA (2000) statement on the nature of science (see http://www.nsta.org/about/positions/natureofscience.aspx) identified science as an enterprise characterized by the systematic gathering of information through observation, the testing of this information by experimentation and other methods, and the production of knowledge about naturalistic concepts and the laws and theories that govern them. This definition also points out that "scientific knowledge is simultaneously reliable and tentative" (para. 3) because it is based on repeated observations, yet is always subject to revision in light of new evidence or knowledge.

Three Components of Science Instruction

Using this definition of the nature of science implies three related components that should form the core of effective science teaching and learning. One aspect is the scientific method itself, which often is taught as a series of steps beginning with questioning, proceeding through data collection, and concluding with interpretation and prediction. Although it is often explained as if it were a flow chart, many practicing scientists would say they do not use all of the steps as taught in school, nor do they follow the steps in a linear fashion. The ability to tailor the application of the scientific method to the needs of a given scientific problem or question is not generally emphasized in K–12 science instruction, although it is a suitable learning objective for high-ability learners and is sometimes mentioned in science curriculum standards.

A closely related aspect of science learning includes what are known as *process skills*; these are the basic technical competencies that underlie the scientific method, including skills like classification, measurement, communication, and inference. Some definitions also include specific techniques or the use of specific laboratory equipment for measurement (e.g., a graduated cylinder or a centimeter ruler) within these broad process skill categories. Process skills can be taught in isolation to build specific skills, or they may be integrated within a broader, project-based approach to provide additional development after basic competency has been developed.

Content knowledge, and especially the acquisition and application of specialized vocabulary, is the third component of science learning. Without a foundational knowledge of the proper terms for things, which is referred to as *remembering* in Bloom's revised taxonomy of educational objectives (Anderson & Krathwohl, 2001), it is difficult to teach or to learn the higher level relationships and concepts that should form the bulk of science learning for students with gifts and talents.

The skills of *analyzing*, *evaluating*, and *creating* occupy the top three levels at the higher end of Bloom's revised taxonomy.

These skills are vital to learning to think like a scientist, which is a primary purpose of science education. These also are the aspects of Bloom's taxonomy that are emphasized in gifted education, which suggests a natural instructional fit between the goals of these two specialized educational fields. Because these objectives (especially *creating*) can be difficult to teach, it is all too common that these higher levels are not emphasized in the schools to the extent that they should be.

Teacher Competencies and Science Instruction

Current best practices in science education emphasize an inquiry approach, and this approach is consistent with the learning motivation framework described previously. Such an approach allows learners to apply their factual knowledge in a manner that forces them to move beyond rote memorization and into higher cognitive processes. In the inquiry approach, science teachers are encouraged to develop learning activities that allow students to gain understandings based in empirical experiences of scientific processes and draw from patterns and relationships found in the natural world. What then does this inquiry approach suggest about the teacher competencies needed in science instruction?

Content knowledge in many fields of science is an ever-evolving target. Although some topics, such as Newtonian physics, have not changed appreciably in hundreds of years, other areas (such as biochemistry or materials science) see new discoveries that require textbooks to be revised annually. To generalize, the content of basic science instruction remains substantially the same from year to year, and a teacher can rely upon his or her own educational background for expertise. However, when working with highly able learners, who may be more inclined to pursue advanced topics in greater depth, the teacher's background knowledge may quickly become both outpaced and outdated. Thus, lifelong and ongoing learning of new scientific content is vital for teachers who work with academically advanced learners.

Fortunately, there are a number of resources available to assist the dedicated science teacher in keeping up to date with new developments in his or her fields of science. Various magazines strive to present current scientific developments to the educated adult reader; *Science News* is one exemplary example in this category. Other magazines range from a more technical approach, such as in *Scientific American, Nature,* or *Science,* to more popularized accounts in magazines such as *Chemical Heritage* or *Smithsonian.* One great way to locate science magazines with the appropriate focus and depth for your students is to browse the magazine shelves at a large bookstore. Current magazines are valuable not only for the teacher's own education; often, they also may be used as a resource for enrichment and in support of individualized research activities by advanced students.

A second and extremely valuable source of ongoing professional development comes in the form of summer programs offered by many colleges and universities. These often involve internships in science laboratories, where the teacher participates directly in cutting-edge scientific research. Universities may receive grants to support the participation of teachers in such programs—they may even pay a stipend to participating teachers. By staying in touch with local higher education institutions, and especially with faculty who work in the area of science education, teachers can maintain awareness of these types of opportunities. Web searches also can be helpful in identifying opportunities that may require additional travel. Although laboratory-based opportunities abound, there are also ample opportunities for teachers to pursue field research experiences that emphasize data collection in rain forests or aboard ships, excavation of important archaeological sites, or engagement in science in other interesting settings.

For teachers in Advanced Placement (AP) classrooms (which are further described in the Improving High School Instruction in Science section), one of the most effective ways of becoming a better AP teacher is to participate in scoring AP exams. The AP exams are scored in early summer, following the exams' administration in May, usually over 2–3 days of intensive work. Although such exam scoring practice is not directly related to updating one's content knowledge, it clearly does lead to greater knowledge of what effective and ineffective AP exam responses look like, and helps teachers gain a better sense of what topics are likely to appear in questions on future AP exams. Developing this area of expertise can lead to more effective teaching and learning.

Finally, one aspect of working with high-ability learners that often is overlooked by teachers is the unique social and emotional needs of these students. Teachers should be aware of, and responsive to, issues such as perfectionism and underachievement that are likely to occur among students with gifts and talents. Awareness of these issues appears to be a particular concern at the high school level, including in Advanced Placement coursework, where affective issues have traditionally taken a back seat to content mastery. There are many ways teachers can learn more about these needs, ranging from participation in discussion groups led by school counselors or talking with former students who have demonstrated resilience, to reading relevant books such as Hébert's (2011) *Understanding the Social and Emotional Lives of Gifted Students*. The inquiry approach to science teaching and learning is valuable because by improving student motivation, the potential to help students overcome affective issues such as underachievement and the negative forms of perfectionism is enhanced.

Finding and Developing Appropriate Curricula

Tensions in Science Education

In public education today, there is a tension between two distinct philosophical approaches to the role of the teacher. In one view, teaching is a mechanistic act in which anyone who is provided with the appropriate curricular resources can be a successful teacher. This view is accompanied by efforts to standardize the curriculum (i.e., to have all classrooms on the same page of the textbook on the same day). This perspective tends to focus on having students meet minimal competency standards, as measured by their performance on multiple-choice tests of grade-level content. Teachers under this perspective are not encouraged to individualize instruction; in fact, they may be actively discouraged from doing so by the threat of unfavorable performance reviews or other disciplinary action.

In the opposing philosophical approach, teaching is viewed as partially an art and partially a science. Specific pedagogical skills, in this view, form the foundation on which effective teaching is built; however, these skills are viewed as necessary but not sufficient to ensure effective instruction. Because even the most effective teacher will work with a different group of learners each year, mastery of teaching is a moving target. The effective teacher selects from an arsenal of skills and techniques, deliberately selecting the ones that are most likely to be successful based on his or her understanding of the learning needs of individual children. Because learning in this view interacts with students' characteristics and teachers' instructional preferences, each classroom at a given level is likely to be at a different place in the curriculum on any given day, even though all classrooms ultimately will have engaged with the desired content in an effective manner by the end of the school year. It is the author's view that this "teacher as professional" approach is the one that must be followed when working with students with gifts and talents.

A second and more general tension in science education has been between an emphasis on science literacy for all learners versus advanced science content learning for those students who show career potential in the sciences. These two emphases are not necessarily mutually exclusive, but as Subotnik and colleagues (2010) have identified, an exclusive focus on science literacy can detract from provisions for an appropriate education for advanced learners. Because many advanced learners will not go on to careers in the sciences, both objectives should be emphasized in educating these children in the sciences.

Standards and Science Teaching and Learning

There has been a substantial amount of attention in recent years devoted to the international competitiveness of U.S. students—or more precisely, their lack of competitiveness, particularly in the areas of science, technology, engineering, and mathematics (STEM). International comparisons of student performance on the Trends in International Mathematics and Science Study (TIMSS) and the Programme for International Student Assessment (PISA) consistently show U.S. students are performing well below the top tier of countries in student performance. The TIMSS (Gonzales et al., 2009) has been conducted five times since 1995 (including its most recent administration in spring 2011). Results from the most recent year available (2007) show that U.S. students' science performance was above the average for all participating countries at both fourth and eighth grade but fell behind students in several Asian and European countries. On average, the science scores of U.S. learners in 2007 were not measurably different from scores of U.S. learners in 1995, suggesting that average science performance has not improved in those 12 years.

The PISA (Fleischman, Hopstock, Pelczar, & Shelley, 2010) is an international comparison of student literacy in mathematics, science, and reading that is conducted every 3 years among 15-year-old students across more than 60 countries. In the 2009 administration of PISA, U.S. students scored at the average level in science literacy, and only 29% of students both in the U.S. and on average across all comparison countries scored at or above Level 4 in this area. Level 4 on this measure represents proficiency in higher order thinking skills in science; in other words, students scoring at this level are able to apply their knowledge and skills to develop solutions to complex scientific problems in a real-life context.

The middle-of-the-road performance demonstrated by U.S. learners in science undoubtedly is due at least in part to differences in the structure of schooling in countries around the world, to differences in the homogeneity of the student population, and to important cultural differences in the value placed on educational achievement. However, it seems likely that this relatively lackluster performance also may be due to the curriculum and instruction we follow for science teaching and learning in U.S. schools.

Curriculum historically has been patched together from competing and partially overlapping standards developed at the state and local levels, mingled with standards developed by national content-area organizations, and as a result what students learn has varied widely from one school to the next. This now may be changing because in the last few years, a majority of states have adopted the Common Core curriculum guidelines developed by the Common Core State Standards Initiative (http://www.corestandards.org) in place of their unique state curricula. These standards address learning through the frame of reading proficiency, with the overarching goal of career and college readiness. Science is treated separately for grades 6–12, while science and all other subjects are integrated within the reading standards for grades K–5. Of indirect interest to science learning, these standards advance mathematics competency in comparison to most states' standards, with the goal of having most learners able to complete Algebra I in the eighth grade. This is important because in many cases, students who have not completed this course as eighth graders will not be able to take the full range of advanced or AP science coursework during high school due to prerequisite mathematics course requirements.

Gifted Models and Strategies in the Science Classroom

Despite years of effort, models and strategies in gifted education are not as well developed as similar models are for areas such as special education. Although there are a wide variety of models and strategies available in the gifted education literature (Renzulli, Gubbins, McMillen, Eckert, & Little, 2009), relatively few of these models have a strong base of research supporting them. In at least one case, the author of a model appears to be the only one to have investigated its efficacy. Many of these models sound appealing, and at first glance may appear to have substantial support, but further inspection may reveal that the support is limited to expert opinions. Relatively few of these approaches are specific to instruction in the sciences, although with further development many of them probably could be applied to this content area.

The William and Mary Science Curriculum

One notable exception to the general lack of research support is the gifted science curriculum units developed by VanTassel-Baska and her colleagues from The College of William and Mary.

As summarized in *What Works: 20 Years of Curriculum Development and Research for Advanced Learners* (http://www.prufrock.com/client/whatworks.pdf), these science units led to increases in students' abilities to plan experiments and apply critical thinking skills, as well as their engagement in the science content. This line of research also has demonstrated greater achievement growth in all school settings for students using the William and Mary units, in comparison to students using the standard science curriculum, and students at Title I schools in particular have shown significant gains on performance-based assessments that emphasized scientific investigation, higher order understanding, and mastery of science content.

The William and Mary science curriculum units use a problem-based learning approach that is aligned with the Integrated Curriculum Model (Feng, VanTassel-Baska, Quek, Bai, & O'Neill, 2005). This model emphasizes the three intersecting dimensions of concept (understanding systems), process-product (using scientific research), and advanced content (science). These units are available through Kendall Hunt and Prufrock Press.

Problem-Based Learning

As the William and Mary units have recognized, problem-based learning (PBL) is among the most suitable general frameworks for curriculum development for high-ability learners in the sciences. PBL originally was developed beginning in the 1970s in response to concerns in medical education, where instructors observed that medical students often had difficulty in applying their comprehensive factual knowledge to the complex real-world task of diagnosing actual patients. Because medical students by definition are high-ability learners, it makes sense that the same approach that works with these learners may also be effective with gifted students at younger ages.

Perhaps the most important consideration in effective problem-based learning is the selection of an appropriate problem.

PBL begins with a substantive problem that is ill-structured, meaning that it is not framed in a manner that allows a single correct answer; the problem must be realistic, yet it also should be complex and multifaceted. The problem topic is consciously selected by the teacher to help students acquire specific concepts and skills. It should be one that students find intrinsically interesting, and it should be an issue for which arriving at one or more solutions will require students to pursue new knowledge. Once students have become familiar with the problem scenario, they work collaboratively to design a strategy for pursuing a solution; they then implement the solution through a combination of self-directed learning, apprenticeship, and collaborative effort with their classmates.

Improving Elementary Instruction in Science

Early and ongoing exposure to science is vital for all learners to develop the problem-solving skills they will need to participate effectively in our technologically complex society. Such repeated exposure to science also is vital for high-potential learners to receive the background knowledge they will need in order to navigate successfully the complex pathways that lead to careers in science and related STEM fields. The National Science Teachers Association (NSTA) has developed an effective framework for elementary science instruction in its position statement on this topic, which is available online at http://www.nsta.org/about/positions/elementary.aspx. Key factors the NSTA identified in this statement include firsthand inquiry as an instructional method; presentation of science content organized into conceptual themes that build on students' existing understandings; approaches that foster a positive attitude toward science; ongoing, research-based professional development to give teachers the knowledge and skills they need to integrate science as a foundational component of the elementary curriculum; administrative and community support for science learning; and ongoing assessment that is aligned with inquiry, process skills, problem solving, and related curricular objectives.

It should be apparent from this summary of NSTA's position and from the Common Core Standards' inclusion of science within the elementary reading standards that science instruction at the elementary level should take a very integrated approach. Unfortunately, in practice teachers often feel that dedicating time to subjects that will not be tested, such as science and social studies, somehow takes instructional time away from the tested core competencies of reading and mathematics. This misguided view all too often leads to the outcome that science instruction is only provided at the grade level(s) where it is tested, when in fact it should be a core component of the elementary curriculum at all grade levels.

Extracurricular Activities Add Interest for High-Ability Learners

Elementary-aged learners can participate successfully in a variety of extracurricular activities that foster a love of science while simultaneously developing both a depth and breadth of understanding about specific science topics. Science fair projects offer a way for students working individually to shine, whereas Science Olympiad offers a team-based experience.

Science fair projects can be an incredible learning experience for elementary-aged children, but they require a long-term commitment from teacher and student alike due to the extensive scaffolding teachers and other adults must provide to help young learners successfully navigate the multiple components these projects entail. Additional keys to a successful elementary science fair experience include choosing a manageable topic (which must be an experiment, rather than simply a demonstration) and keeping on top of the documentation that science fairs affiliated with the Intel®

International Science and Engineering Fair® will require (see http://www.societyforscience.org/isef for details).

Science Olympiad (http://soinc.org) is another remarkable program that features standards-based learning opportunities for students at all grade levels and competitive opportunities beginning as early as third grade. Team competitions provide a broad array of options that can be matched with the interests and learning strengths of individual team members, and as with science fairs, opportunities for travel to regional, state, and nationally competitive venues are available for successful teams. Information on founding a team is available on the organization's website.

As NSTA pointed out, both ongoing professional development and administrative support are necessary for effective science instruction in the elementary grades. Administrators in particular can help ensure that science content forms a core part of the school's curriculum at all grade levels and for all learners. Related actions, such as supporting extracurricular clubs and other activities in science or recruiting relevant guest speakers to the school, also allow administrators to demonstrate their support. Supporting science-related field trips and developing relationships with local colleges, universities, and industries to provide exposure to science career pathways can also help strengthen science learning for all students.

Although some children will demonstrate more aptitude and greater interest in science than others, all students are capable of learning fundamental scientific content and processes and all learners should be given the opportunity to do so. High-potential learners are especially likely to become passionate about one or more particular interest areas in science, but *children and young adults may not yet know what these areas are.* Someone who loves hydrogeology, for example, is not likely to have learned about it in elementary school or during K–12 coursework at all. Part of the effective teacher's job is to raise awareness of the broad range of content that science careers might include. Reading broadly about science helps the teacher find interesting career paths to share with his or her students.

As mentioned previously, extracurricular activities can enrich science learning at the elementary level. Although such activities often are completed outside of the regular school day, they might also be implemented, at least in part, within the regular instructional time. Providing such activities within the regular school day is especially important for students from low-income households, as students in such settings may lack the material resources or parental scaffolding necessary for their efforts to yield a successful outcome. As a science fair judge for many years, this author finds it tragic when a student has developed an outstanding project idea, has shown the initiative to complete it without adult assistance, and has taken a unique approach to understanding the topic, but then is not recognized with an award simply because he or she lacked the simple materials needed to conduct and present the research effectively.

Choosing Instructional Content for K–5 Science

Choosing content often seems to be a source of difficulty for elementary teachers who want to integrate science into their instruction. Although state or local curriculum guidelines often can provide some input, many times these are written broadly about concepts (e.g., "change" or "development") and do not provide details about how these concepts might be addressed in classroom instruction. This is a good thing! The "teacher as professional" view (see Tensions in Science Education subsection in the Finding and Developing Appropriate Curricula section) supports teachers' autonomy in selecting the curriculum they feel is best for teaching any given objective. So, how can teachers get started in this process?

Some professional organizations offer access to high-quality lesson materials with membership in the organization; for example, the National Science Teachers Association offers teacher-focused journals at the elementary and other levels with membership. There also are many other resources that NSTA and related organizations make available to the public. For the important topic of evolution, NSTA provides a publicly available web page with links related to teaching about this topic (see http://www.nsta.org/publications/evolution.aspx?lid=pub). The Public Broadcasting System (PBS) offers online courses about teaching evolution that are based on its programming on this topic (see http://www.pbs.org/wgbh/evolution/educators/course), and a report from National Public Radio (NPR; http://www.npr.org/templates/story/story.php?storyId=4630737) offers state-by-state discussions of legislation affecting the teaching of evolution. The NPR story could be used to provide English or social studies content in a unit integrated with the other science lesson resources.

There are literally thousands of science lessons available online at no cost, but the instructional quality of these lessons varies widely. There also are lesson plans available from publishers, often bundled with a particular textbook, but these too vary widely in quality. In both cases, lessons often are not suitably differentiated to meet the needs of high-ability learners in the heterogeneous classroom. The Curriculum Studies Network of the National Association for Gifted Children annually sponsors an award for effective curriculum for students with gifts and talents, and their award criteria (see http://www.nagc.org/index.aspx?id=1204) and rubric provide a useful framework within which curriculum may be evaluated. Also, prepackaged assignment grading rubrics often are heavily based on completion (i.e., Did the student hand something in?) rather than on the quality of student work (i.e., Did the student do his or her best work?). For advanced learners, it is preferable to have fewer assessments but with a stronger focus on the quality of students' work.

In choosing content for elementary science instruction, many of the mathematically based physical sciences (e.g., physics, chemistry, or biochemistry) are not practical due to the math mastery they require or due to safety issues involving chemicals or laboratory apparatus. There are some exceptions, such as the physics topic of simple machines, in which both the math (e.g., force times distance) and the equipment for inquiry learning (e.g., pulleys, the inclined plane) can be quite straightforward and therefore appropriate for use at the elementary level. Although the physical sciences sometimes can be difficult to adapt to the elementary level, the natural sciences remain extremely practical as topics for science instruction.

If your school has any kind of outdoor area on its grounds, this opens up ample opportunities for learning about living organisms and the natural environment they inhabit. Although school in most cases is not in session during the summer season when many garden crops would be harvested, a school garden still can prove extremely valuable as an interdisciplinary and inquiry-based learning resource. Of course, class gardens and other outdoor resources can be relevant to science instruction at all grade levels, but they are especially inviting to elementary-aged learners because of their immediacy and their hands-on nature. Bean plants and investigations of their light and soil requirements are a staple of elementary science instruction, but teachers working with high-ability learners should proceed with confidence beyond beans to lessons involving other living organisms and their environments.

Teachers often are less familiar or less comfortable with organisms other than plants, which is unfortunate because a variety of insects can be used in science instruction even when the school has limited or no access to the outdoors. Caterpillars and their life cycle are so widely used that they are almost a cliché in the elementary classroom, but a broad and interesting variety of other invertebrates also are commercially available. Crickets are easy to maintain, and they usually can be obtained locally at shops where fish bait is sold; ask at the store to find out who provides them, so you can get in touch with the grower to ask for tips on maintaining them in the classroom. Crickets are featured in a number of children's stories, from *The Very Quiet Cricket* to *Pinocchio*, helping students to make learning connections between science and literature. Crickets also lend themselves to investigations in which students apply and extend their mathematics skills. Measurement skills are one obvious application (e.g., How long are they? How small can a hole be for them to still crawl through it? How fast do they walk?), but higher level questions also are appropriate (e.g., After students measure that their cricket can walk 40 cm in one minute, can they determine how long it would take for the cricket to walk 2 meters? Do crickets prefer to walk in well-lighted or dark places, and in what ways might someone measure how brightly lit a habitat is?). Such investigations with a focus on inquiry can address many aspects of effective instruction for advanced learners, while simultaneously meeting mandated accountability requirements for instructional time spent in reading or mathematics.

Other slightly more exotic insects also are available, and may be especially appropriate for advanced learners who already are familiar with the basics of the insect life cycle as demonstrated by caterpillars and butterflies or by an ant farm. One very beneficial and interesting insect is the praying mantis, which can be ordered from sources such as Carolina Biological Supply (http://www.carolina.com/home.do) in the form of an egg case from which dozens of tiny mantises will emerge. These young should be fed fruit flies and soon separated from one another, as they also will eat their siblings. Mantises and other insects lend themselves to a variety of lessons on topics ranging from observing and describing life cycles or feeding habits, to investigations of behavior and responses to environmental stimuli. A list of easy-to-raise insects for the classroom also would include fruit flies, meal worms, and a variety of others that may be ordered.

To sum up, elementary science instruction can and probably should be integrated with instruction in other core content areas. Relevant curriculum standards support such integration, and student interest increases when learners can apply their strengths in writing or mathematics to science activities. An integrated curriculum also allows teachers to devote instructional time to science content without neglecting the primary areas in which student performance will be evaluated (i.e., reading and mathematics). Science activities that focus on the local environment and on inquiry-based approaches in the natural sciences are especially well suited to the elementary classroom.

Standards in Grades 6–8

The Common Core Standards begin treating science as its own content area (i.e., no longer integrated within the reading standards) in grades 6–8. Areas emphasized include summarizing science texts and determining their central ideas or conclusion, analyzing the author's purpose and organization in texts, and following multistep procedures in performing scientific tasks. The standards also emphasize determining the meaning of specific technical terms; integrating textual and visual presentation of information (i.e., as charts or graphs); distinguishing factual information from speculation, judgment, or opinion; and comparing other sources of information (e.g., experimentation or video) to textual presentation of the same topic.

By middle school, students have become far more capable of following instructions and examples than they were as elementary learners. More complex investigations become possible as a result. Students also show substantial cognitive growth during the middle school years, including a developing ability to engage in abstract reasoning, which permits teachers to assign projects that have increased complexity and require greater independence. Competitive extracurricular venues such as science fairs recognize this growth, as students in the middle grades and higher usually may attend district or state-level competitions that often are unavailable to elementary-aged learners.

Affective Issues in Grades 6–8

At odds with the developing reasoning skills that middle school students display is an increased focus on social and emotional issues during these years. Asynchronous development, in which students appear to act like small adults in some respects yet like small children in others, is increasingly evident especially among academically gifted learners. Students at this level may begin to perform (or not perform) based on whether or not they like or respect the content-area teacher; middle school seems to be the age range where students' dislike for their teachers first becomes apparent, as elementary-aged learners (as a rule) love their teachers.

Middle school learners display a broader range of physical and emotional development than students at either the elementary or high school level, and their discomfort with this asynchrony may be compounded by the larger number of teachers and students they interact with. The typical middle school model involves a team of three to four teachers, one for each content area, with students moving in groups through the sequence of content-area teachers. This model is effective because it allows teachers to work in their area of content strength, although if the school does not group students by ability at the school level (Gentry & MacDougall, 2009) then it remains difficult for teachers to differentiate instruction despite their content expertise.

Some middle schools recently have begun to shift to smaller, two-teacher teams using teachers who hold licensure in two different content areas; interdisciplinary lessons are easier to implement when the same teacher has training in and responsibility for both areas. Middle schools and elementary programs alike also may have a gifted education specialist teacher who works with multiple classrooms either within or across grade levels. Collaboration between the regular classroom teacher and the specialist can provide greater opportunities for developing extra-curricular activities, individual investigations, and differentiated learning experiences for students within the general classroom setting.

What Is Differentiated Instruction?

Differentiation involves providing varied levels of instruction that are designed to meet students' individual needs as learners. In general education settings, differentiation is used to make content accessible for students in special education who are included in the mainstream classroom, often via collaboration between a general education teacher and a resource teacher. In gifted education, the goals are similar, but the process is based in knowledge of the specific personality traits and learning behaviors that tend to be characteristic of gifted and advanced learners. These traits include a fondness for abstract or complex ideas; the ability to learn with fewer examples or less repetition than other learners; and a low tolerance for errors or omissions by others, sometimes in conjunction with overly high self-imposed standards for the student's own work.

Differentiation for students with gifts and talents should incorporate preassessment measures that identify what content students already have mastered, along with alternate activities (different work, not simply more work) for students whose pretest results show they already know the content of a planned unit of instruction. Alternate activities should incorporate modifications to four aspects of instruction: content, product, process, and learning environment:

- Content modifications may include increasing the complexity or degree of abstractness, offering a greater variety of content, and incorporating study of the methods of inquiry used and the important people within a given discipline.
- Product modifications may include having products address real problems and real audiences, such as peers and professionals in the discipline, in the evaluation of student products, giving students a choice of product format from a variety of options, and emphasizing the collection and analysis of new data in student products.
- Process modifications should emphasize offering open-ended and discovery-oriented activities that involve the application of information and explanations of the process of analysis, rather than being limited to knowledge acquisition alone, providing a faster pace of instruction and a greater variety of instructional methods, and fostering guided autonomy in learners' choice of activities.
- Learning environment modifications should include providing a student-centered rather than teacher-centered setting that is open to new materials and ideas, emphasizing flexibility in grouping methods and in the degree of mobility students are allowed within the classroom, and incorporating assessments that address the strengths and weaknesses of ideas, rather than only whether they are correct or incorrect.

Selecting Science Content in Grades 6–8

As in elementary school, the quality of science instruction in the middle grades is highly dependent on the individual teacher. Curriculum standards in science tend to be more focused than they were at the elementary level, but they are not yet as narrowly focused on a specific subject as they will become in high school. This means that there is still a substantial amount of room within which teachers can develop their own approaches to meet the standards.

One temptation that middle school teachers should resist is the urge to draw science content for advanced learners directly from high school lessons. This is for two reasons. First, important content details often are inadvertently omitted in an effort to make the lessons suitable for middle school learners. Second, students will feel that they "already did this" when they see the same content again in high school; they will not be as interested as if they were seeing it for the first time, and they may not attend to the nuances of the high school lesson as a result. Middle school science content for advanced learners should be different; otherwise, why do it? Moving the advanced learner directly into the high school course would make far more sense than simply presenting a watered-down version of high school content in the middle school classroom.

Middle school science curricula usually are organized into one of two broad approaches. One of these is a spiral design, in which (in theory) the same content is revisited each year but in greater depth with increasing grade level. The success of this approach depends on close collaboration between teachers across grade levels, and on the effective application of diagnostic assessments to determine what students have retained from prior years' instruction. The other approach tackles a specific discipline each year (e.g., physical science in sixth grade, life science in seventh grade, and Earth science in eighth grade). Either approach can be consistent with gifted education perspectives on curriculum such as the Parallel Curriculum Model (Tomlinson et al., 2009).

Although students are far more likely to have a dedicated science textbook in middle school than they were in elementary school, middle school science textbooks traditionally have suffered from several drawbacks, and poor content is only one of these (see, for example, the discussion of a middle school physics lesson by Hubisz [2003], on pp. 4–6 under the heading "A Basic Experiment"). Textbooks at this level often are written by committees of curriculum developers rather than by an individual scientist, so they may not have a coherent voice; a variety of errors may creep in because different individuals were responsible for different portions of the book. Middle school science textbooks also have shown a tendency to focus on flashy graphics to grab student attention, rather than on science content, and they have been criticized for jumping from topic to topic (i.e., having lots of breadth) without providing sufficient detail about any single topic (i.e., lacking depth of coverage). Finally, because of the way they are marketed, textbooks usually are written to satisfy the requirements of one or more specific large markets (e.g., Texas or California), so they may not be well matched to the curriculum standards or instructional needs of other states. Textbooks also are subject to an approval process, usually by an appointed board at the district or state level, before local schools may select them. This process can be extremely political, as Nobel laureate Richard Feynman (1985) documented (see the authorized online excerpt describing his experiences at http://www.textbookleague.org/103feyn.htm).

The ideal solution to these drawbacks would be to avoid using a textbook in the middle school science classroom, or at least to use it only as one resource among many rather than as the sole source of information in the classroom. Unfortunately, for many teachers (especially those who are just beginning their teaching career), their own limited expertise with the content may lead them to rely heavily on the textbook and its associated resources (which may include a bank of test questions, answer sheets, laboratory activities, and so forth). A heavy reliance on premade content moves teaching back toward the mechanistic end of the spectrum, with a corresponding reduction in the attention devoted to differentiation of instruction to meet the individualized learning needs of students.

How, then, can teachers reduce their reliance on the textbook? In the long term, gaining content expertise through summer internship programs and other strategies noted earlier will help in accessing up-to-date content and bringing new ideas into the teacher's repertoire. More rapidly, reading a variety of science lessons on a given topic, whether online or in professional magazines such as *The Science Teacher* (see http://learning-center.nsta.org/browse_journals.aspx?action=issue&thetype=free&id=10.2505/3/tst11_078_05) can be useful for developing one's expertise in specific instructional content and how to convey it effectively. Developing an individualized repertoire of effective lessons will require several years of effort, and piloting a variety of approaches in the course of this process is how pedagogical expertise develops; it is a career-long process in which there is always more for the teacher to learn.

In many districts, professional learning communities comprised of teachers from different teams (within a school) or even across middle schools have been established to help teachers in planning lessons within a given content area. If a professional learning community is not available, teachers should consider pulling together a collaborative coalition of colleagues for this purpose. With advances in web-based communication such as video conferencing, it is now possible to create such communities with former university classmates, colleagues one meets at professional conferences, or other interest groups, without being limited to participants from the local geographic area. Such long-distance communication is vital for teachers in small and/ or rural schools, who may be the only teacher in their area who works with academically advanced learners or with specific science content areas.

In summary, although middle school presents multiple opportunities for delving deeper into science content, these opportunities are not always realized in practice. Students at this level want to exceed the expectations of teachers whom they respect, yet high-ability learners in particular may be sensitive to shortcomings in the teacher's content knowledge that diminish this respect. Much of the burden of developing expertise in science content and its effective delivery to learners rests on the individual teacher, and textbooks written for the middle school market are not as helpful as they should be in helping teachers deliver content that is technically adequate and appropriately differentiated for high-ability learners in science.

Improving High School Instruction in Science

Standards in Grades 9–12

The Common Core Standards follow the same reading-based approach to science in grades 9–12 as for grades 6–8. Competencies become more complex, but continue to focus on the ability to understand textual material, and to translate from textual to (and now also from) visual or mathematical formats such as charts or equations. The high school level also adds an increasing emphasis on the ability to evaluate scientific texts, both for internal support and in comparison to external sources of evidence. The ability to follow complex instructions to conduct experiments and to synthesize information across varied sources and perspectives also are emphasized at this level.

How Is High School Science Different?

Grouping practices. Most high schools already group students into two to three instructional levels at the classroom level, usually based on their prior subject-area performance in middle school or in previous high school coursework. Such grouping generally is a good thing, as not every student is both willing and able to meet the demands of high-level courses in science (and also in mathematics, as completion of selected mathematics courses is a prerequisite for some advanced courses in the physical sciences). Teachers are able to move at a faster instructional pace in classrooms with advanced learners by reducing the amount of time spent on remediation and repetition; this faster pace decreases advanced learners' boredom, thereby improving their motivation.

Grouping also comes into play in a second way. Although much scientific work in real-world settings is based on collaborative effort, science learning at the high school level usually requires a substantial component of individual effort (of course, collaboration in real-world settings is with individuals who already have proven their ability to achieve individually, as demonstrated by their successes during many years of formal education). The increased expectations for individual performance at the high school level may come as a shock to students who have become accustomed to a middle school learning environment that focused heavily on group work. Although some students may experience difficulty making the transition to assuming greater responsibility for their own learning, others (often high-ability students) may welcome the change because they no longer feel like they have to do other students' work in order to receive a good grade in group activities. Interestingly, in postsecondary education, many programs (notably engineering) once again emphasize group work for solving complex real-world problems.

Although ability grouping reduces the range of ability levels within a class, differentiation frequently still is necessary to provide all learners with an appropriate education (see the sidebar on What Is Differentiated Instruction? in the middle school section). Books such as *Differentiation That Really Works: Science* (Adams & Pierce, 2012) offer helpful strategies to aid teachers in middle and high school grades in differentiating their instructional delivery. Differentiation may involve approaches such as choice boards, tiered lessons, and learning contracts; accessing these collected approaches in a ready-to-apply format allows teachers to devote more of their planning time to decisions about appropriate content and strategies for presenting it.

Extracurricular involvement related to science learning becomes increasingly important in the high school and college years for students who wish to pursue scientific and research careers. Teachers can contribute by helping organize and staff science fairs and other competitions, as well as school-based clubs and related activities. Some different types of out-of-school science learning opportunities are provided in Thinking Outside the Box.

Thinking Outside the Box

Although they are important at earlier grade levels, out-of-school science experiences assume even greater importance at the high school and college levels. Subotnik (2005, p. 61) has identified several general forms that such experiences may take:

- *Kitchen science.* This refers to science investigations conducted informally at home alone or with friends. Subotnik noted that these generally involve chemistry or rocketry; the portrayal of Homer Hickam in the movie *October Sky* illustrates some aspects of this form. These activities are self-selected, so interest is high, but without the involvement of a mentor, the depth of learning and ability to connect it to higher education or career opportunities may be limited.

- *Olympiads and other test-based competitions.* These are competitive events that develop the ability to answer quickly. Taken alone, they may not be a good model for the usual science process, but they can be a good way to develop factual expertise in a field of study.

- *Science research programs.* These provide high school and undergraduate students with the opportunity to engage in actual professional work in a field of study. Subotnik noted that sustained involvement through at least the second year of college is likely to lead to a successful transition into a research career in the sciences.

- *Intensive summer courses.* These are specific, competitively selected opportunities in various areas of the sciences, usually offered for 1–10 weeks during the summer. In the U.S., university-affiliated talent search programs (Lee, Matthews, & Olszewski-Kubilius, 2008) are major sponsors of this type of opportunity, although states and universities also sponsor a variety of programs specific to the sciences. Programs are characterized by challenging coursework and opportunities to interact socially with peers who share similar interests. Subotnik noted that costs of attending can be high, and that participants may be disappointed when they compare the summer program environment with the regular school experience when they return in the fall.

- *Science-related clubs.* The content and organization of these may vary widely based on members' interests. Such clubs can provide opportunities for sharing scientific interests, for accessing advice on problems, and building mentoring relationships between newer and more experienced members.

Advanced Placement coursework. Most high schools now offer Advanced Placement (AP) courses, which are college-level courses that are taught by high school teachers. Students receive a grade just as in a regular high school course, but at the end of the year they also take a national exam based on the AP content. Students who score well enough on the exam can receive college credit for their work. Credit from AP courses can help high-ability learners complete college sooner, or can make room in their college schedule for the exploration of additional elective courses in areas of interest.

High schools' policies for who can take AP courses have become more inclusive over the past few decades, and in some states more than one in five high school students now take at least one AP course before they graduate. In many high schools, AP courses are open to anyone, although policies for introductory courses like AP Human Geography may be more open than those policies for more technically demanding courses such as AP Physics. There is some tension among AP teachers between excellence and access, as some feel that allowing all interested students into AP has led to decreased rigor and a slower instructional pace in these courses. Course content in the AP classroom often is very standardized; nevertheless, AP exam pass rates can vary widely across teachers and schools.

Affective Issues in Grades 9–12

The complexity and specificity of science content increases drastically beginning at the high school level, and this may affect student performance. High-ability students who have not felt challenged in their prior coursework may not have developed appropriate study skills, and as a result they may flounder the first time they encounter rigorous coursework. Teachers and parents should keep a close eye on the performance of students who seem to be sailing through their coursework without effort, and should be ready to provide appropriate scaffolding in study skills as needed, if or when these learners encounter unexpected difficulties. For some learners, this may not pose a problem until they reach college or even graduate school.

For learners who are twice-exceptional (i.e., students who have gifted-level strengths in one area, but who also have a learning disability or attention disorder), the disability may become more apparent in high school. As content demands increase, the student's strengths may be no longer sufficient to compensate for the area of disability; this means that the disability's impact on performance may become evident for the first time at the high school level.

Learners who were in pull-out gifted programming during their elementary and middle school years may have gaps in their prior knowledge, especially if their school's gifted programming emphasized enrichment rather than acceleration. Teachers should be aware of this possibility and make available resources or remediation to fill in any instructional gaps observed. Diagnostic testing is appropriate for determining where content gaps may be evident. Because of these students' strong academic ability, it will take relatively little time for them to catch up to the performance levels of classmates.

Online coursework is becoming increasingly available, especially at the high school level. Many programs are run at the state level, such as the North Carolina Virtual Public School or the Florida Virtual School, while others may be organized in the form of charter schools or even in-house, sponsored by a specific school district or other entity. Depending on how they are structured, these courses can offer ample opportunities for students to accelerate their learning. Because high school science courses often have laboratory components that can be difficult to replicate in the online environment, it may be advisable to take English or social studies coursework online to make room in the student's schedule for additional science coursework in the face-to-face setting. Online courses also may be appropriate for students who are uncomfortable working in close proximity to other learners in traditional settings, or for students who have fallen behind due to family or medical difficulties during the school year.

Academic underachievement may also become more of a problem at the high school level as grading and attendance policies grow increasingly strict. At the same time, students' increased freedom, including the ability to drive and to date, may detract from their attention on scholastic performance. It can be quite difficult to distinguish underachievement that is due to education-related causes (such as boredom due to lack of challenge) from low achievement that simply may be due to a lack of interest or other focused priorities outside of the school setting; in either case, these will interfere with the sustained and focused attention that developing science talent requires.

Conclusion

Becoming an effective teacher requires a commitment to ongoing growth and reflective development—a far more time-consuming and strenuous route than most individuals outside of education realize. In this volume, those salient issues have been highlighted that influence one's understanding of science teaching and learning in K–12 schools. A listing of resources has been included both within and at the end of this volume for the interested reader. It is hoped that by raising awareness of the components of effective science education programming for gifted and academically advanced learners, more children will develop the knowledge, skills, and inclinations to pursue careers in the sciences.

Resources

American Association for the Advancement of Science (AAAS)
http://www.aaas.org
AAAS is a nonprofit association whose mission is "to advance science, engineering, and innovation throughout the world for the benefit of all people." AAAS publishes the influential academic journal *Science*. Through its Project 2061 initiative (http://www.project2061.org), AAAS developed the standards document *Benchmarks for Science Literacy*, which lays out a vision of what all students should know and be able to do in science, mathematics, and technology by the end of grades 2, 5, 8, and 12 (see http://www.project2061.org/publications/bsl).

American Science & Surplus
http://www.sciplus.com
American Science & Surplus sells an ever-changing variety of hobby-sized surplus materials including electric motors, lenses and other optics, and lab supplies but also including the ever-popular rubber chicken. Many of their items are ideal for putting together science fair project apparatus or other inventions, but

it's the tongue-in-cheek descriptions of each item that make their catalog and website a consistent source of entertainment.

Carolina Biological Supply
http://www.carolina.com/home.do
Carolina Biological Supply is a useful commercial source for insects and other living organisms for classroom use. It also sells lab safety equipment, materials and lessons for AP Biology, and a wide variety of science curricula developed for grades K–8.

Common Core State Standards Initiative
http://www.corestandards.org
This website includes an interactive map showing which states have adopted these standards, and provides links to download the Common Core State Standards text in PDF format.

Khan Academy
http://www.khanacademy.org
This is a nonprofit website designed to provide a free self-paced education to people everywhere through carefully constructed instructional videos. At the time of this writing, the site offers nearly 3,000 educational videos that cover extensively K–12 and some college-level mathematics (from arithmetic and Singapore Math through differential equations); sciences (including chemistry, physics, biology, organic chemistry, astronomy, computer science, and healthcare); history; art history; and finance. Additionally, useful for the advanced learner are test preparation videos focusing on solving sample problems from tests including the SAT, California Standards Test, and GMAT.

MAKE Magazine
http://makezine.com
MAKE is a quarterly publication that focuses on teaching the reader how to build innovative projects that often utilize components scavenged from other commercially available items. Projects and the magazine's occasional contests emphasize cre-

ative thinking and developing an understanding of how things work. Although many projects focus on electronics, particularly interfacing equipment with computers using micro-controllers, others recreate historical machinery. Recent how-to articles have included making a specially modified home fish tank for keeping jellyfish, reproducing the 19th-century theater technology known as the limelight, and building an electronic temperature controller to convert an ordinary Crock-Pot into a yogurt incubator. Difficulty levels range from do-this-in-your-backyard to far more complex, but with such wide variety that everyone from children to professional engineers will find projects they are capable of doing in each issue. The magazine's website highlights content drawn from current and previous issues, and provides video-format instruction and links to purchase the sometimes-obscure parts for some of the featured projects.

National Academies Press
http://www.nap.edu
The National Academies Press publishes government reports and books on topics related to science and health policy in the U.S. Many of its more than 4,000 publications, including the National Science Education Standards, are available as free PDF downloads.

National Science Teachers Association (NSTA)
http://www.nsta.org
NSTA publishes a variety of periodicals addressing science teaching at specific levels from elementary through college. The website includes links to breaking news related to science teaching and learning, highlights the organization's leadership role in developing and disseminating relevant standards in science, and promotes upcoming conferences. Specific sections of the site include information for parents and new teachers, and even a few competitions and grants available to teachers and students. NSTA also maintains an extensive collection of professional develop-

ment resources related to science teaching, many of which are free.

The Planetary Society
http://www.planetary.org
The Planetary Society is a nonprofit, nongovernmental membership organization that exists to promote space exploration and to advocate for scientific missions that seek to learn more about the solar system and to look for conditions favorable to life beyond Earth. Through its publications and related outreach efforts, the Society seeks to generate public involvement in the discovery process. The Society's current executive director is the well-know science educator and television show host, Bill Nye.

Smithsonian Institution's National Science Resources Center (NSRC)
http://www.nsrconline.org
The NSRC was founded in 1985 with the goal of improving the learning and teaching of science for all students. The NSRC's Leadership and Assistance for Science Education Reform Center offers a framework designed to assist schools and districts in making effective reform efforts in K–12 science education, and the NSRC also produces and disseminates research-based science education curricula. The NSRC's website also has a page of student and parent resources, which includes a list of science centers and museums organized by region.

Society for Science & the Public
http://www.societyforscience.org
The Intel® International Science and Engineering Fair® is the governing organization for most science fairs at the state and local level. The fair's nonprofit parent organization, Society for Science & the Public, also sponsors the Broadcom MASTERS (Math, Applied Science, Technology, and Engineering for Rising Stars) competition for middle school students, and publishes breaking scientific discoveries for a general readership in the

periodicals *Science News* and *Science News for Kids*. *Science News* is a great way to keep up with current events in a wide variety of scientific fields.

References

Adams, C. M., & Pierce, R. L. (2012). *Differentiation that really works: Science.* Waco, TX: Prufrock Press.

Anderson, L. W., & Krathwohl, D. R. (Eds.). (2001). *A taxonomy for learning, teaching and assessing: A revision of Bloom's taxonomy of educational objectives* [Complete edition]. New York, NY: Longman.

Eccles, J. S., & Wigfield, A. (2002). Motivational beliefs, values, and goals. *Annual Review of Psychology, 53,* 109–132. doi:10.1146/annurev.psych.53.100901.135153

Feng, A. X., VanTassel-Baska, J., Quek, C., Bai, W., & O'Neill, B. (2005). A longitudinal assessment of gifted students' learning using the Integrated Curriculum Model (ICM): Impacts and perceptions of the William and Mary language arts and science curriculum. *Roeper Review, 27,* 78–83.

Feynman, R. P. (1985). *"Surely you're joking, Mr. Feynman!": Adventures of a curious character.* New York, NY: W. W. Norton.

Fleischman, H. L., Hopstock, P. J., Pelczar, M. P., & Shelley, B. E. (2010). *Highlights from PISA 2009: Performance of U.S. 15-year-old students in reading, mathematics, and science literacy in an international context* (NCES 2011-004). Washington, DC:

U.S. Government Printing Office. Retrieved from http:// nces.ed.gov/pubs2011/2011004.pdf

Garn, A. C., Matthews, M. S., & Jolly, J. L. (2010). Parental influences on the academic motivation of gifted students: A self-determination theory perspective. *Gifted Child Quarterly, 54,* 263–272. doi:10.1177/0016986210377657

Gentry, M., & MacDougall, J. (2009). Total school cluster grouping: Model, research, and practice. In J. S. Renzulli, E. J. Gubbins, S. K. McMillen, R. D. Eckert, & C. A. Little (Eds.), *Systems & models for developing programs for the gifted & talented* (2nd ed., pp. 211–234). Mansfield Center, CT: Creative Learning Press.

Gladwell, M. (2008). *Outliers: The story of success.* New York, NY: Little, Brown.

Gonzales, P., Williams, T., Jocelyn, L., Roey, S., Kastberg, D., & Brenwald, S. (2009). *Highlights from TIMSS 2007: Mathematics and science achievement of U.S. fourth- and eighth-grade students in an international context* (NCES 2009-001 Revised). Washington, DC: National Center for Education Statistics. Retrieved from http://nces.ed.gov/pubs2009/2009001.pdf

Hébert, T. (2011). *Understanding the social and emotional lives of gifted students.* Waco, TX: Prufrock Press.

Hubisz, J. L. (2003). *Choosing middle school science textbooks: Is North Carolina failing its students?* Raleigh, NC: North Carolina Education Alliance. Retrieved from http://jove.geol.niu.edu/ faculty/kitts/GEOL301/hubiszscitextreview.pdf

Kanevsky, L., & Keighley, T. (2003). To produce or not to produce? Understanding boredom and the honor in underachievement. *Roeper Review, 26,* 20–28.

Kim, K. H. (2008). Underachievement and creativity: Are gifted underachievers highly creative? *Creativity Research Journal, 20,* 234–242. doi:10.1080/10400410802060232

Lee, S.-Y., Matthews, M. S., & Olszewski-Kubilius, P. (2008). A national picture of talent search and talent search educational programs. *Gifted Child Quarterly, 52,* 55–69. doi:10.1177/001698620731115

Matthews, M. S. (2006). *Encouraging your child's science talent: The involved parents' guide.* Waco, TX: Prufrock Press.

Matthews, M. S., & McBee, M. T. (2007). School factors and the underachievement of gifted students in a talent search summer program. *Gifted Child Quarterly, 51,* 167–181. doi:10.1177/0016986207299473

McCoach, D. B., & Siegle, D. (2003). Factors that differentiate underachieving gifted students from high-achieving gifted students. *Gifted Child Quarterly, 47,* 144–154. doi:10.1177/001698620304700205

Morisano, D., & Shore, B. M. (2010). Can personal goal setting tap the potential of the gifted underachiever? *Roeper Review, 32,* 249–258. doi:10.1080/02783193.2010.508156

National Science Board. (2010). *Preparing the next generation of STEM innovators: Identifying and developing our nation's human capital* (Report #NSB-10-33). Washington, DC: National Science Foundation.

National Science Teachers Association. (2000). *NSTA position statement: The nature of science.* Retrieved from http://www.nsta.org/about/positions/natureofscience.aspx

Neber, H., & Schommer-Aikins, M. (2002). Self-regulated science learning with highly gifted students: The role of cognitive, motivational, epistemological, and environmental variables. *High Ability Studies, 13*(1), 59–74.

Renzulli, J. S., Gubbins, E. J., McMillen, K. S., Eckert, R. D., & Little, C. A. (2009). *Systems and models for developing programs for the gifted and talented* (2nd ed.). Mansfield Center, CT: Creative Learning Press.

Ryan, R. M., & Deci, E. L. (2000). Intrinsic and extrinsic motivations: Classic definitions and new directions. *Contemporary Educational Psychology, 25,* 54–67. doi:10.1006/ceps.1999.1020

Simonton, D. K. (1999). Talent and its development: An emergenic and epigenetic model. *Psychological Review, 106,* 435–457.

Simonton, D. K. (2003). Scientific creativity as constrained stochastic behavior: The integration of product, person, and process perspectives. *Psychological Bulletin, 129,* 475–494. doi:10.1037/0033-2909.129.4.475

Subotnik, R. F. (2005). Out of school science programs for talented students: A comparison. In P. Csermely, T. Korcsmaros, & L. M. Lederman (Eds.), *Science education: Best practices of research training for students under 21* (NATO Science: Science and Technology Policy, Vol. 47). Amsterdam, Netherlands: IOS Press.

Subotnik, R. F., Tai, R. H., Rickoff, R., & Almarode, J. (2010). Specialized public high schools of science, mathematics, and technology and the STEM pipeline: What do we know now and what will we know in 5 years? *Roeper Review, 32,* 7–16. doi:10.1080/02783190903386553

Tomlinson, C. A., Kaplan, S. N., Renzulli, J. S., Purcell, J. H., Leppien, J. H., . . . Imbeau, M. B. (2009). *The parallel curriculum: A design to develop learner potential and challenge advanced learners* (2nd ed.). Thousand Oaks, CA: Corwin Press.

Michael S. Matthews, Ph.D., is associate professor and graduate program coordinator for academically/intellectually gifted in the Department of Special Education and Child Development at the University of North Carolina at Charlotte. Dr. Matthews held academic positions with the Duke University Talent Identification Program and the University of South Florida before moving to the faculty at UNC Charlotte in 2008. Dr. Matthews is a former laboratory chemist and high school chemistry teacher who also has worked in a variety of summer program settings teaching science topics to students in grades 2–10. He is a board member of the North Carolina Association for the Gifted and Talented and a former board member of the Florida Association for the Gifted, as well as an active member of the Research & Evaluation Network of the National Association for Gifted Children and the Research on Giftedness, Creativity, and Talent special interest group of the American Educational Research Association. He has written two other books with Prufrock Press, as well as more than 15 peer-reviewed journal articles and a variety of book chapters and other publications related to gifted and high-ability learners. He is coeditor of the

Journal of Advanced Academics, and serves as an editorial review board member for three other gifted education journals. Dr. Matthews' research interests include content learning in science, mathematics, and second language acquisition; gifted education policy; the assessment and identification of learners from diverse backgrounds; and motivation and underachievement among gifted and high-ability learners. In his spare time, he enjoys teaching his children about nature and the history of technology.

Printed in the United States
by Baker & Taylor Publisher Services